Q&A Kids

MATERIALS

AMY CHAPMAN ANGELIKA SCUDAMORE

WINDMILL BOOKS

Published in 2026 by Windmill Books,
an Imprint of Rosen Publishing
2544 Clinton St.
Buffalo, NY 14224

First published in Great Britain in 2026
by Wayland

Editor: Sarah Peutrill
Designer: Lisa Peacock

Some of the text in this book was
first published in Fact Cat: Materials
by Izzi Howell

Cataloging-in-Publication Data

Names: Chapman, Amy, author. | Scudamore, Angelika, illustrator.
Title: Materials / Amy Chapman, illustrated by Angelika Scudamore.
Description: Buffalo, NY : Windmill Books, 2026. | Series: Q & A kids | Includes glossary and index.
Identifiers: ISBN 9781725396258 (pbk.) | ISBN 9781725396265 (library bound) | ISBN 9781725396272 (ebook)
Subjects: LCSH: Materials--Juvenile literature. | Materials science--Juvenile literature.
Classification: LCC TA403.2 C437 2026 | DDC 620.1'1--dc23

Printed in the United States of America

CPSIA Compliance Information: Batch #CSWM26
For Further Information contact Rosen Publishing
at 1-800-237-9932

Find us on

CONTENTS

Can you spot the plastic toy robots in this book? There are 13 to find, not counting me.

MATERIALS

Q. What are materials?

A. We use materials, such as wood, plastic, and metal, to make different objects. A book is made from paper. A blanket is made from wool.

Some objects are made from more than one material. This boy's shirt is made from cotton (fabric) and plastic (buttons).

THINK ABOUT IT

What do you think the labeled things might be made from?

Windowpane
Curtain
Bed
Blanket

PROPERTIES OF MATERIALS

Q. Are all materials the same?

A. No, there are many materials in the world, which is really useful because they have different properties.

The different properties of a material help us describe it. For example, glass is hard and smooth. A ceramic plate feels hard, but it is not strong. It will break easily if you drop it.

Tests can help us to decide which properties a material has. We can use our hands to feel that a brick is rough.

Some materials have different properties, depending on how they have been treated. When wood is cut from a tree, it feels rough. However, if you rub wood with sandpaper, it becomes smooth.

FIND IT

Can you find two hard metal objects and two soft objects?

CHOOSING MATERIALS

Q. Why aren't houses made out of sweets?

A. Sweets are tasty but they are not strong enough to hold up a house.

When you are making an object, it is important to choose a material that has the right properties. For example, an object that needs to be hard, such as a knife, should be made from a hard material, such as metal.

A chair needs to be made from a strong material, such as wood, so that it can hold the weight of the person sitting on it.

Objects made from the wrong material will break easily or will not be useful.

THINK ABOUT IT

Something went wrong here! Some of the things have been made from the wrong material. What should the things be made from and why?

Tent
Lamppost
Umbrella
Bench
Shoe

SOLIDS, LIQUIDS, AND GASES

Q. When does water become ice?

A. Water changes into solid ice when it cools and freezes.

Materials can be solids, liquids, or gases. Solid materials keep their shape. Liquids can flow into the shape of any container you put them in. Gases float in the air.

Metal and plastic are solid at room temperature. However, if you heat them to a very high temperature, they will melt into a liquid. When they cool down, they will become solid again.

THINK ABOUT IT

Ice has melted from the roof. Why might that be?

NATURAL MATERIALS

Q. Where do materials come from?

A. Some materials come straight from nature. Wood is a natural material. It comes from the trunks or thick branches of trees. You need a strong metal tool, such as a chainsaw, to cut down trees to get wood.

People can change natural materials in workshops and factories. Wool is collected from sheep. The wool is cleaned and spun into wool thread.

Precious stone

Clay pot

THINK ABOUT IT
Which of these natural materials have not been changed in any way?

Plank of wood
Rock
Sand
Shell
Bamboo
Ball of wool
Chalk
Soil

HUMAN-MADE MATERIALS

Q. What are human-made materials?

A. Materials that are human-made can't be found naturally in the world. Human-made materials are created from natural materials and changed into something quite different, for example:

Paper is made from trees by grinding wood down into tiny bits and mixing it with water.

Plastic is made from oil and other materials which are heated and changed into plastic.

Glass is made from sand and other materials. When the sand is heated to a high temperature, it melts into a liquid. When the liquid cools down, it forms glass.

A clay pot begins as a lump of damp clay. It is shaped into a pot and baked in a hot oven to change it into a hard pot.

FIND OUT

Can plastic be turned back into oil?

Tree to paper

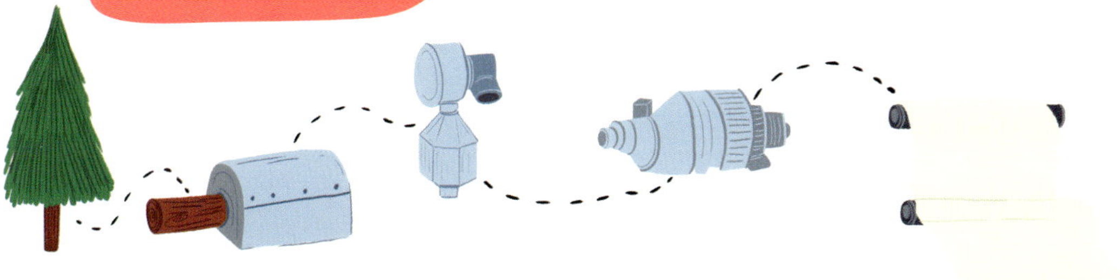

Oil to plastic

Sand to glass

Clay to pot

CHANGING SHAPE

Q. Can solid materials change?

A. Yes, we can change the shape of some solid materials by bending them or twisting them.

Forces affect each material in a different way. If you bend aluminium foil, it will keep its new shape. That makes it a good material for wrapping around other objects.

Rubber is a stretchy material. If you push or pull rubber, it will change its shape.

However, it will go back to its original shape if you stop pulling or pushing it.

THINK ABOUT IT

When the girl sits on the rubber ball, the ball is squashed by her weight. What will happen to the shape of the ball if the girl stands up?

LIGHT AND MATERIALS

Q. Why can I see through glass?

A. Materials like glass and water are transparent. This means light can travel through them.

Opaque materials are things that do not let any light through at all.

Most materials, such as metal and cardboard, are opaque. You cannot see through them.

Translucent materials let light through, but not all of it. You cannot see clearly through translucent objects.

FIND IT

Can you find one transparent object, two opaque objects, and one translucent object in the picture?

ABSORBENT MATERIALS

Q. Why do my feet get wet if I jump in a puddle wearing socks?

A. Materials act in different ways when you put them in water. Some materials, such as the fabric in your socks, absorb the water and become wet.

We use a towel to dry wet hair. The fabric towel absorbs the water.

THINK ABOUT IT

Oh, dear, there's been a water spill! Which of these will help to mop it up? Which will not?

If you hang up your wet towel, it will dry, ready for the next time you need it.

WATERPROOF MATERIALS

Q. Umbrellas are made of fabric, so how do they stop me from getting wet?

A. Not all fabrics are absorbent. Some, such as the nylon in your umbrella, are made to be waterproof.

Waterproof materials do not absorb water. The water sits on the surface of the object or slips off easily.

Rain boots are often made out of rubber, another waterproof material.

Birds spend a lot of time in water. They have waterproof feathers so that they don't feel wet and cold! They make them waterproof by spreading their feathers with special oil that they make themselves.

FIND IT

Grace has to choose waterproof materials from this selection. Can you help her?

Rain boots
Rain jacket
Sponge
Leaf
Rubber gloves
Sock
Umbrella
Wool
Rubber ducks

ELECTRICITY AND MATERIALS

Q. Is electricity a material too?

A. No, electricity is a kind of energy that we can't see. It powers things like lamps. We know it's there in objects like electrical cables.

Electricity can pass through some materials, such as some metals, like copper and iron. These materials are called electrical conductors. They are used in electrical cables and plugs. Most materials do not let electricity pass through them.They are called electrical insulators. Plastic, wood, and glass are examples of electrical insulators.

THINK ABOUT IT

We wrap metal cables in plastic so that the electricity cannot escape. Why don't we wrap metal cables in wood or glass?

Ask your grown-up about ways to stay safe around electricity.

HEAT INSULATORS

Q. Why do I have to bundle up in cold weather?

A. Fabric hats and scarves keep you warm in the cold. This is because they stop your body's heat from escaping.

Some materials, such as fabric and wood, are insulators of heat. They do not let heat pass through them.

LOOK AT IT

How many sorts of fabric heat insulator can you spot?
Oh no! Someone has forgotten to bundle up warm. Can you find them?

HEAT CONDUCTORS

Q. Has anyone invented a wooden frying pan?

A. No! Wood burns easily so that would not be very useful!

Heat moves easily through some materials, such as metals like steel and aluminium. These materials are good conductors of heat.

Pans need to be made from a material that conducts heat. This is so that the food inside the pan heats up and cooks quickly.

THINK ABOUT IT

Saucepans often have plastic handles so that you don't burn your hands on the hot metal. Is plastic an insulator or a conductor of heat?

QUIZ

1. Which of these is a property of glass?

a) bendy

b) smooth

c) absorbent

2. Rubber is a stretch material. True or not true?

a) true

b) not true

3. Plastic is a human-made material. True or not true?

a) true

b) not true

4. Which word describes a material that light cannot pass through?

a) transparent

b) translucent

c) opaque

5. Fabric absorbs water. True or not true?

a) true

b) not true

6. Which material isn't an electrical insulator?

a) plastic

b) copper

c) wood

Quiz answers

1. b – smooth
2. a – true
3. a – true
4. c – opaque
5. a – true
6. b – copper is an electrical conductor